Territory

Territory

Gigi Marks

Silverfish Review Press
Eugene, Oregon

Acknowledgments

Some of these poems appeared in the following magazines: *Brain of Forgetting*: "Bedtime." *Cider Press Review*: "Dandelion." *Connotation*: "Some Days" and "Everyone Can Learn Something." *Damselfly*: "On Hands." *North American Review*: "Rooster." *Permafrost*: "Fuel." *Poetry Monday*: "New Year," "Live Without" and "Mushrooms." *So to Speak*: "Before Walking." *Southern Poetry Review*: "Seasonal Stream." *The Fourth River*: "Familiar" and "Reminders." *Raven Chronicles*: "Territory" and "This Cradle is Rocking." *The Voices Project*: "Goodness in the World," "Early June" and "One Seed." *WomenArts Quarterly Journal*: "On the Surface of My Skin."

Published by
Silverfish Review Press
P.O. Box 3541
Eugene, OR 97403
www.silverfishreviewpress.com

Distributed by
Small Press Distribution
800-869-7553
spd@spdbooks.org
www.spdbooks.org

Library of Congress Cataloging-in-Publication Data

Names: Marks, Gigi, author.
Title: Territory / by Gigi Marks.
Description: First edition. | Eugene, Oregon : Silverfish Review Press, 2019.
Identifiers: LCCN 2018032720 | ISBN 9781878851703 (pbk.)
Classification: LCC PS3613.A757 A6 2019 | DDC 811/.6--dc23
LC record available at https://lccn.loc.gov/2018032720

9 8 7 6 5 4 3 2 First Printing
Manufactured in the United States of America

Contents

Hand in Hand

Territory

Green

Fuel

Monday, I felt the touch
of death lifted. There was too much
wood left over in the woodpile
to be worried about the last frosts,
about the cold month of May,
the days just stained with green.
There were new leaves everywhere.
There was fuel enough for every bit
of life, it seemed.
I put my bare toes into the dusty soil,
and when I leaned over to wipe them,
the blood was swimming in my veins,
and I could see the world from
between my knees: it was alive,
leafy, trembling, turning green.

Mud

Truly we are made of mud,
made from the slick warm
mud that tells us that our
parents are alive, that lets us
grow in form and later
shape ourselves, after they
have finished with us.
And later still, when another
puts a hand to us, grains
still wet and fluid, we find
ourselves unmade again,
and ready for that other making.
There is a moment of discovery—
when we pause and notice
what we are and will not be
for long—and then there is
the tug and slip that follows,
back to the ground and
all the mud that made us.

Not a Single Word

All squirrels depend on the
cavity in the tree, the open
wound that holds before rot
sets in, the roots still pulling
water from the soil, the regular
surge and flow of sap from
ground to furthest tip
and highest points. And then
there is the seed to gather,
back to the ground they chatter
even on this day when you and I
don't speak, since morning,
not a single word.

Goodness in the World

The egg cracks open to see
mid-day: so much light pours in
that one is almost blinded.
And perhaps it would be better
to be blind at that single moment
when there are angelic voices all around,
and when the voices become
her mother's first sigh, her father's
first response. The room darkens.
Another child has been born
and what changes will settle,
happen again, as before.

Before Walking

Before your feet would carry
all the weight of yourself,
before your toes and heel
pushed off against the ground
and walked and walked and
settled, flattened, stood,
and I only held you in my arms,
before you balanced upright,
before you stopped and sat
and put feet up to rest,
they were wrapped in one
soft piece of skin, that drifted
up ankles and legs, all in
one piece that shimmered
with newness. Toes at the end
that could reach into the air,
the arch not formed yet but
curving like a shell does
into the rounding of the sea,
the heel barely more than
the beginning of the whole foot,
shining beside the other one,
also new. They were the back
and front of you before walking,
the bottom and top not ready
yet for the near constant stepping on,
holding you up, bearing your weight.

Two Boys

Two boys walk to the creek
to look for rocks, fossils,
feathers, things to hold and fill their hands.
They find sticks that float down-
stream; they let them go from the banks
and follow them to where they wait and catch.
Then the release begins again,
and the boys go, and go
and they have not looked up
until they are farther than they thought,
and when they hold the sticks, rescued
from the creek, so far from home,
I see for a moment a look of fear
surface on their young faces.

Herself

One moment she is asleep
the next she wakes, but does she?
what thoughts are only hers when
the sky behind her head
holds the sunrise, the singing of birds
and the rooster crowing?
Only after she has bent herself
at the knees, unfolded folded hands
and put her lips together to stop
an ongoing current of air, only
after she hasn't thought a thing yet,
then she begins to rise and think again.

Some Days

Think of the trees,
the sycamore, dogwood, sugar maple,
a stable oak, a twisted pine, and
see the leaves or needles
as clearly as we see the fingers on our hands,
and see the depth of their roots as possibilities,
as directions to follow, and that we are
directional ourselves, leaning one way
and staring with green eyes toward
leafy branches. When I say I am
no longer troubled by your closeness,
I am thinking of the trees, the way
trees grow, branches overlapping,
shade richer underneath two than one of them,
each grown accustomed to the roots that are
spreading together underground.

Familiar

I want you to be untricked.
I want you to listen carefully
to the day birds and night frogs and
I want you to eat directly from the swollen
garden. Do not be fooled by beauty.
I want you to press grain stalks
between your palms, feel its fine feathers,
and talk to the woodpecker
who is eating beneath tree bark,
and I want you to ask forgiveness
for the dead squirrel, mid-line of
the road, its one open eye
rimmed with blood.
I want you to bend down to your
own feet and recognize the bends
and shapes of toes and arches
and I want you to be familiar
with the regular sense of season
and the rhythm of friendship
and the breath of love.

Everyone Can Learn Something

Tadpole quivers under algae,
the pond breathes, I've got
a breath of water stuck in my throat;
the reeds hold turgor but still bend
to the wind. When I clear the way
for air, the tadpole has disappeared,
the reeds stand still. Who is there
holding witness to our breath?
Now that I am looking at the surface
of the pond, I see my reflection,
hair dark, my body a bright, light object.
It is only me and no one else
who sees that I am breathing again,
who sees the tadpole underwater come
close again when things are quiet.

What I Was

I was once that vine
merged to the tree, lucky to have chosen
the one who would support me and
still grow. I was once in the wintery
stream, flush and full, the fallen leaves
breaking up against my hips
and arms. I was once so fine
a line I could fold the entire sky
at its horizon, my body rich and
important, the visible element, and
you, beside me, I knew you felt it.

In Close Reach

The nest of birds woven
into tall grass has failed
its birds: visible to the pond-
muskrat, and too easily reached.
We'd seen the eggs, then the hatchlings
huddled together. The red-winged
blackbird used to call us back from looking.
Did the muskrat waken its attention
When it heard that warning?
Did the parents know who might eat its young?
I've heard the birds who have lost theirs,
and I keep mine nearby,
careful, underwing, when they let me.

Clover

just begins to put its big
head up, a white cloud,
green-tinged with the idea
of seed. it is ringed by others;
it is rarely alone. it doesn't see
with eyes; its feet just under
surface weave through the grass.
It shudders under any weight,
from breeze or bee, or the shadow
of the cherry tree, but we think
we know it isn't scared.

Territory

On the bridge of my finger,
the ant crawls, doesn't stop when I place it
down on the ground. From the grass,
one comes across the plain skin
of my leg and doesn't stop, follows its
way over. I am the territory of a country
that is so easily traversed. I am soaked
in familiar smells, enough to keep an ant
at ease in its pace. I wear grass stains
on my knees and pine needles stuck here
in my hair, and there is a similar language
we have—dirt, grass, leaves—between
our separate bodies, small and large.

In and Out of the Shadows

Do Not Forget

I trade awarenesses—
notice one in place of another—
so that the geese who are
eating the waste grain in
the cut wheat field for several days
replace the secretive glimpse
of the green heron by the pond.
And so days in a row go by
where I am counting on
the flock of geese to be there,
while small frogs of the pond
do not forget the constant hunger
of the heron that I have forgotten.
And you, I notice you,
your eyes only grow green again
when the geese have flown.

Lifesaving

In the dark green reflecting
pool that deep water makes
of itself, there is only a little
effort you must make to keep
your head at air level. The air
is dangerous when you struggle;
it slips away, and it becomes
in your confusion the dark water
and enters your mouth in
a swift clear current.
I see the swimmer struggle
and then he catches another
breath of air, one that steadies
him, guides him back, lets
him float in the water,
the roundness of his belly,
his toes, his cheeks bubbling
on the surface while the rest of
the world becomes a green ring
growing around that deep pool.

In

Spring is in the young dog
running the brown field,
stretching her head out, her legs out,
and is in the snowflakes
aloft in silver air, and even though
the cold is stirring up in currents
as we walk and hold hands to keep warm,
spring is in our feet, finding edge of sole
and rise of toes and the great block
of our heels so we notice how alive
they are, just as we take each step
and stride in our boots, in the field, in spring.

On the Surface of My Skin

I caught the bee's stinger
near my lip, felt the heat
spread across my face, and then
a certain numbness.
My lip swelled, brightened,
the venom underneath
followed the swath of tissue
overlying jaw and cheek.
My skin was a blanket, a red rose,
the expanding sky, and the richness
of disfigurement awoke conflicting
desire: look at me, touch the swollen
surface, notice the sheen of stretched
skin, and let me, if I can, hold
my face in my hands and hide.

Boy

He is not alone. I have cared for him
and seen him grown almost to a man.
This other boy is still young,
and I care for him as he grows,
like and unlike his brother:
feet, hands, their legs, their necks,
their sparkling eyes, their hearts
that beat under their ribs.
They are not alone: I see them smile,
see their tempers rise and fall, watch
them think, see my sons sleep at night,
or in the morning. Their bodies are their own,
even as I have cared for them and
I know that they are not alone.

Reminders

When the warmth is withheld,
the trees hold buds a bit longer
suspended in their branches, unleafed,
and remind me of the cold,
how they must wait for spring.
There are other reminders:
when the rain, with its dark saturation
carries the chill before spring
can begin. When the world is spongy,
when anything empty
is instantly filled with the cold water
and then when it rises, not waiting
any longer, and overflows.

Look Back

Remember where you've come from—
skin of a parent's hand, smell of hair that comes
to mind. Resist the pattern of not remembering
so that by traveling back to the dark color of a night
alone, the bright sky of a single day, the path is just
as easy ahead as it is behind. Remember often
enough so that each step forward you are closer
to remembering that first cry near birth.
Tomorrow I will not be here to look into your eyes.
But look back. I am always there, near
to that moment you can find when you were born.

This Cradle Is Rocking

This cradle will keep rocking
us back and forth, in the foamy
waves, in the salty tides,
and in the chilly water,
I am as much a child as my
child swimming alongside
me. The cradle rocks,
waves lift us, we reach the sandbar
further from shore and rise up
from the depths. We are
light on our feet, we run
in the shallows, we are the top
part of waves, the surf,
and look, a gull has freed itself
from a cloudbank and come to
tell us the news, but it is as if
we are just recently born,
we are too new to listen:
we submerge, let the sea
rock us, bring us to shore.

Blackberry

I've got the thorns of it
tracked down my leg,
but it doesn't matter because
the dark fruit has been
plucked between my fingers
and filled my basket.
Later, I will remember
how you looked nearby
in the mirror of the pond,
where I could cup your face
like a single blackberry
in my empty hands.
When the scratch raises
and scabs on my leg
there is still the tug
of the dark juice when I was
eating from the thorny bush
and there is still your image
rising from the water near me.

You

In the steady roll
of sound, the child's song is
steady in her throat, the birds
in tree branches, the shouts across
the field that speak to the wheat
and later the gigantic throb
of the combine that tells it of its end.
You can follow the voices that
may seem lost in this vast sea:
and you can walk out to hear
the harvest in progress, the snap
of grain from staff, the ground
rumbling, the engines calling,
the chorus of birds from the edge,
but you must come back to me.

Handwork

Two cedar waxwings have
feathers that are a pink-colored,
brown-tinged gray; that is
a rich, sweet color, I say
to myself; it shifts the space
between my ribs to accommodate
a fuller breath, and my heart
feels bigger, and one of the birds
has the tippet feathers pure
yellow to border its back,
and both have the familiar
tuft that is shared with the cardinal
and jay, and they lie together
on the macadam road, which
heats up in the middle of the day
and shimmers a bit as it
softens. I move each to the grassy
shoulder, my hand is a stretcher,
my hands can do only this.
My daughter who is with me
says, oh no, did they get hit by
a car, why are you moving them,
oh they are so beautiful, the two
of them, at least now they are
back in the grass.

In the Shadows

These are the griefs we do not see:
unheard cries in the woods, unknown
losses, a heap of animal troubles
that shadow our own without our
knowing. You and I are outside when
the damselfly lifts from the bowing
reed, when tomorrow's rain comes early,
and we rise to go home, leaving the grasses
where we sat flattened and bruised.
You join the shadow of the clouds,
the length of your body dark and
unsteady, trembling on the path ahead.
I walk behind, and you cannot hear me
call out, but you turn as if you do,
looking in the rain for me.

Sunflower

You can barely imagine the force
that holds the heavy flower up, how
steady it is to wind, driving rain:
it is a hollowed trunk, not a stem;
it is like wood, but it is more
simple and green.
And the flower tracks the sun,
grows seeds rich in its oils
while it rests easy up there.

Early June—Hawkweed and Fleabane

Up the road, where a field is bright with hawkweed,
I remember other times I have passed by
less quickly, and that if I want to see
the bunched up flower, the frayed petal edges,
I need to stop, bend at the knee,
and not remember what it looks like.
And when I see nothing except for the green
shade and the ripe grass and the yellow flower
on its fragile stem, I see there's fleabane close by,
with light ray petals, so pretty, and a stem that bends
over with the near weightlessness of its pink flowers
and clear green leaves as if, on this spring day,
it is this kind of attention that tires it.

Offspring

Dirt on foot, on nails, a bruise another.
Follow the leg up, a scratch, the round hill
of a bug bite, the skin ripped where a scab comes,
lifted, off. A dreamy eye, knees and palms
where grass shows itself as crushed green juice,
where hair is only to brush back, away
from face, and where is the animal
who knows any better the look of her young?

Peony

In the house, there are few things to be aware of:
the light is muted compared to the days of growing,
the complete darkness of a cloudy night
that passed over its closed budding,
the ferocious sun when it rose and unshaded glowed
and pulled these petals outward.
And the breezes here are no high wind;
the passersby stir the air but do not shake these
petals much, the fans constant but untroublesome,
unlike the gentle whispers of the bees and wasps
and beetles flying past, and the heavy air that,
lifted in a change of weather, could almost be the end
of a flower. Touch is what it lacks the most, inside,
so different from when the dark small figures of the ants
would crawl, fine-legged, up stem and over sepal
and petal, or when the other leaves and flowers
brushed against each other, responding to the storm.
Here, the flower fades as slowly as the others in the field.
Later, when it is touched with a sleeve's edge,
then a cat's indifferent walk, it sheds its petals
before it can see what happens next.

One Kiss

I hate the shimmer of betrayal,
the metal taste of it.
Everything warns me—
you don't even have to speak.
The single dandelion with white
seeds, the driveway flat with gravel,
the slope of wind. A bee knows, too:
back to the hive, hurry, hurry;
there's nectar somewhere that
no one else will want to drink.

Moth Wing

The moth begins its newest flight
without its body (eaten by a swallow, perhaps)
when there is a breeze that lifts
one tip of its one earthbound wing,
that lifts the entire thing but cannot
keep it aloft for long.
The wing is not as delicate as you might think;
it is thin and light but full of earth
and many of its colors:
brown dirt and darker mud
and still darker coal, outlined by the color
of bright sand and the yellow of the sun.
When the moth falls
flat on the ground, there it stays;
without the breeze that made it fly again.

Daylilies

On the way past the school
the road is lined with daylilies
flowering, looking past the black
pavement with their orange faces,
so hopeful, open, and hiding
nothing. The children aren't there
to see the summer blooms that look
for them: in the July days
they've left the crowded roads;
they are in the woods where
other animals are living,
scuffing up the litter left by trees
or down by the lake
that glitters under the sun.
The school is an empty house,
without an echo, left behind,
and those flowers will be gone
by September. For now, they will
be the children, looking out
for whatever there is in the sun,
and closing up at night.

Where We Live

Gray Tree Frog

There is, in the middle of the day,
no great need for this call
but it is irresistible, sometimes,
to speak out in the spring.
I think of what the voice
can express, and then without thinking,
it almost tumbles out on its own.
In the shade, out of the glaring sun,
the moist waves lift from the newly-
watered plants in their pots,
and there is no need for rescue here,
there is just the unurgent call that
foretells the night: when he will call,
consistently if he needs to, when he will
sing for you until you come to him.

Thanksgiving

The grasses were high and drying
and the fenced-in field held
the near flightless birds right before us,
and my small daughter's hand was in mine.
I kept her upright, she kept me upright,
the haze of misty autumn sunshine
hung around us, and so many birds,
hazy with white feathers, welcomed us
with the sounds of their nature,
so we held out our free hands
to offer tops of grasses and stalks of weeds.
In two weeks, they'd be food for Thanksgiving,
but we saw they were alive and soft-
throated, bareheaded, massed before us
eating near the wire of their fence,
near the food of our hands.

Ready

The lazy dog sweeps
the hearthstones with her tail
and rolls her eyes back into
afternoon sleep, heart beating
in her furry chest,
legs piled on the floor.
But when the coyote calls
at night, she is awake
and racing past the door
I open for her, and
in the evenings when deer
wander past the cornfield
she is ready to chase them back.
My sense of alertness is often
two steps slower than hers,
I notice after she knows.
But sometimes I am the one to tell her—
go, go, chase them back from
the house, and what I say
feeds the smell or sound
of the trespasser into her sense.
She comes back later, settles
by the woodstove, paws sometimes
clacking on the stones, if
the chase follows her there.

Windchime

This is not the flute the rain plays or
the bell-like songs of leaves clapping;
this is the chime of metal on metal
in the wind: it is not the aura of memory,
mother or lover kissing you softly like
a lullaby. It is the breeze that has
been there all day, and now in the evening
lets you know it is there—it is sound and
movement, the music of metal on metal
ringing, hollow, loud enough, perhaps,
to wake you from your dream of it.

Blessing the Bus

You will begin your journey here,
although we know the journey
is always beginning:
the bus will wait, door open, driver ready
to accept the passenger, the tires high
and thick, the glass dark with reflection.
And I will send you off with
the familiar arms, the kiss, everything
you need to take a seat down a row of seats,
and you will wave goodbye to me.
The road will rise and fall, and
the engine will kiss the air with its smoke
and noise, and it will get you and
the others where you need to go.

One Seed

We are born to be
buried, to start our lives in dirt
with light filtering through in bits
or not at all. Once
we are planted there
then we will break our hulls
and send out first green shoots,
a leaf, our first pale roots.
Some of us lifted, once,
into the air on silvery threads
made for floating and traveling,
found a place to fall down to,
a place to grow on earth.
Sometimes we wait a long time
for rain, for heavy spring waters
to drain enough. Sometimes
we are so close to the end
that we put our new green stems
on the ground, wilted, and our recovery
waits for another day.

Sometimes

For more than a week, the hawk
perched on one of the oversized
hay bales in the field; sometimes
I watched its watching. Other times,
its shifting leg to leg or preening
its powerful body. And the goldenrod
had faded; only a few purple asters
still bloomed around the edge—
it was that time of year.
Some hawkweed, yellow and lanky,
but starting to go, too.
Sometimes a small notion gets
fixed into the mind, can be
carried for days without it
growing weight or changing size,
can become its own small territory there,
distinct with its own height and breadth.
Each time I went past the field
I saw the hawk, even when it left
and I knew it wouldn't be coming back.

Where We Have Lived

The stiff shelf of fungi on the fallen trunk
could be the dull paper in your hand,
the whiteness showing nothing to you,
or it could tell you something about
what it has been, when the force that
drove it out of the tree and into
the light of the forest also pulled
that tree down to become closer
to the earth. Nothing here is insubstantial.
It is not insubstantial although
it has grown lighter as it has aged,
less dense, full more of the air
than of fruiting, of spores and such,
the elements of living.
Its attention is ringed by its own
borders; it has grown to its far
reaches, and you can note the colors
that may be pale but are also complete.
It is bright enough, still, to show you
where the ground begins, and where
we are above it, and where we have lived.

On Hands

The rows aren't endless
but the picking is, and each berry
grows bright red in the fingers
of my hand, and redder still before I put it
in the bucket. The sun heats
and sweat builds on my shoulders
while the plants seem to tremble in the hazy air,
and each leaf shivers when I touch it.
As the first hour ends, my back
begins to ache, and my hands balance me
more often on the ground, between
berries, while I take my time.
And I hear you before I see you,
to surprise me with your lips
on my salty neck, interrupting my work,
and I drop the ripe berries that are
in my hands to kiss you back.
But you aren't here.
Your presence at the row edge is just
the sparkling hot sun, which shifts the air.
So my hands don't empty, then, for you.

On Knees

Not clean bright moons,
not just outlined or traced in dirt
but covered and caked in dirt—
the dusty dry dirt of the ground outside.
I can picture where you must have been,
fixed to the cleared ground,
planting the new apple trees, bare root,
carefully, where the slope of hill
is gentle but there, enough
to tip you over when you are working,
if you aren't holding firm.
On your stable knees, with the hole dug,
to be filled in around the straight
alignment of the tree that is slender
and so new in your hand. On your knees,
so that you can place the dirt around it.

Alone

In the sun, I've become like the green bullfrog
that floats on a ragged patch of algae
in front of me, hot, warming its whole body
in the accumulating heat of greenery,
mottled and marked.
My skin with its branching arms and legs
asks for no compliment
but for feeling more of the sun;
and even when the bullfrog
begins to hum right now, with my
standing before it, I know it is not
for me, but for the rich wonder
of the world we are in. No one else
is watching here, and the moment
I dive into the water, so does the bullfrog.

Yes

Yes to the scratch, the dustbath,
to the pecking of feed and the finding
of bugs to eat, and yes to the noise and
the roosting on perches at dark
and the laying of a near-round egg
that sits in the wooly bed of straw
in the morning, and yes to the one eye
at a time that sees then shifts
to the other to look at the ground
where there is a seed, a vibration,
something else to cackle and cluck about.

In Garden

Under a foot of snow,
there are mice who live under
a pile of weedy detritus left there,
and there are stretches of time
when they might not be at all hungry
because they doze in that coldness
with old seed inside them.
And here is more snow falling,
piling up on their close weedy
home, calling them out in
weaving paths for a chance
to find the fallen branch
of red winterberries, if they run beyond
the border of the garden home.

Six Deer

One of us is slower in the new deep snow
and almost trips, moving, trying to keep up.
The next step is deeper, so now
one of us is almost falling, catching a long
branch of prickers that hang on and rip
a little skin beneath the winter coat.
Eyes widen, there are new tears,
and new burrs find old burrs,
mid-leg, to hold onto, in a clump.
It is enough to make one of us
stop, look up with an unfocused, teary eye and
see, not the rest of us who are on the broken path
ahead, but a group of six deer getting ready
to leave the woods and cross the snowy field.
Tall, tall, then there are the smaller ones,
the smallest, and the one who sees them
calls to the rest of us to look.
They take the field and are gone before
we know it, except for the one who stopped and saw.

Valentine's Day

My love gave me new green thread
for a dress I had set aside
to hem, and later
wound the bobbin for me.
Is it strange that in a field of
colors in the sewing box that
no green had come close enough
to match? or that it is a green
so similar to my love's eyes,
a color I couldn't find a name for?
Later, I will try the hemmed
dress on and see the green
thread running at the edge.
Few things last forever, but
there is more than I may
ever need left on the green spool.

Rooster

He is inside the coop,
keeping his call inside himself.
The door opens, and the rust of his voice
speaks just enough to follow
the hens out to eat. The cold morning
has no repeated crow to listen to,
the air hurts the ear that is uncovered
to hear what might be called but
isn't coming. He is placid, quieted
further by the strong wind
that picks up by mid-day,
and before the sun—in its weaker form—
has gone, he's on his roost.
The sound then is just the hearts
of all those birds together keeping
them alive while the cold settles in.

Exterior/Interior

There's a rotted board on the outer wall,
it separates along the grain,
old splinters softening in response to water and air;
and I can hear the weather that wants to come inside.
Inside, the wall that isn't broken holds
along the squirrel's tunnels, the mouse's nest:
listen to their movements in the echo of tap
and scratch, from behind the solid wall.
Yes, yes, the animals are there, alive,
and it is so easy to decide to live with them,
to wait along with them for the repair:
another day to remove the damaged wood,
to measure board, to cut and finish,
to keep the wind and weather out.

Earth Day

After last night's fever recedes—
her over-pinkened cheeks, her glassy eyes
illuminated with heat—a paleness remains,
and she doesn't wake from the soft blanket
that shapes itself to her worn-out body
for long enough to see today's scattering
of violets on the ground—purple, yellow, white—
or the new flowers on strawberries that
have thrown off their own sleep for this.
The fever isn't gone; it blurs the corners
of the room and draws a gauzy curtain
at the window, and the gray trunks
of the trees beyond sink into the new green
oblivion that will grow up around them.
Her hand is light and empty and stays,
settled in its place, and her head has fallen
on the pillow, heavy but not with thoughts of this.

Hand in Hand

Bedtime

In the thunder and lightning that comes
after being born, I didn't sleep;
I stayed awake, thinking of you.
Outside, in the storm, the poppies
swelled with seed, a pair of ducks sank
lower in their nest, and the dark road
washed clean. When you woke in
the fear of the storm, I told you,
sleep, sleep. I was awake, and I could not
think of a time before you were born
and I didn't tell you this.

Bare Root

Instead of the soil that grew it,
there is just air, the clean white
lines of roots that trail
downward from sapling-tree:
and because ground is ground
wherever they find it, the roots know
where they belong, but once
they've been uprooted like this,
do they know the way to get back down?

Snow Day

Here, it is all
snow drift and snow pack
and weight that makes
the shovel heavy.
And high piles and deep snow banks
and an end to any hurry.
The wind is white, it lifts,
then comes back down
to earth to settle.
What isn't white is gone:
can't show itself or
is hidden in the shadows.
And what isn't here
at all is winter's end
that waits in tomorrow's
wet, black puddles.

Mushrooms

Two plucked after the grass unfroze
from a thick frost. Before the thaw, each fallen leaf,
each stem of grass was rimmed with pearls of ice,
sparkling, and a dull background coating on its surface.
The mushrooms are opaque. Having grown
straight up, they are now leaning, first
in hand, then brought inside. Leaning one on the other,
both unblinking. One is brown, one is
whiter than the other. They collapse on the table,
a ragged foot won't hold them up.
There's a shadow beneath them.
There are the dark pleated sections
of their undersides, there is an expanse
of smoothness that says nothing.
There is no sound from these soft forms
except a whistle, an exhale, a chirp
while they arrange themselves and settle here.

Live Without

Just like cup and bowl and spoon
have that roundness made for holding
so we have formed that shape
again with arms and lap and hands
to hold the things that have needed
the cradle of our bodies. Mine
has the wideness of a chair, a bed,
the sea itself, a vastness that when
it is emptied seems to want some
explanation. And yours asks
the question, too: how does it go,
to live, now, without?

Seasonal Stream

I am too sick this year to cover
the ground I usually do; the ways
I part with my hand and tread with
my feet are less tried: I'll walk
around the garden, kick a path into
the unmown grass up to the pond,
see all the ways the wind catches
at cloud edges, like fingers
ripping shreds of cotton plants.
I have half the breath I've had,
and the things I want to see
I sometimes see only in my mind—
this year, I know the stream within
the woods runs full of clear, cold water,
touching bare roots and open bank
with surprising swiftness.
And that it toys with ice, but will not
freeze yet, and when I reach there,
it will perhaps be solid, frozen,
under an inch of new draped snow.
Not now, but when I might move further,
a month or two from now,
perhaps, or in the spring.

I Am

I have been the one who
kneels down to bad dreams
holds the child's hand or
brings him or her into bed with us.
I have been the bridge between
that fear and the safer
sleep of easy dreams
that leave the face clear and soft.
Sweat on that hairline smells
like fruit or milk, and while
I have been so close to soothe
I can tell you also that child's breath
is sweet as honey once
the nightmare passes.

To Dig

The day began with a hole to dig,
a wide well for the trimmed roots
to find a home to grow in. The sky
was a bright bowl overturned,
round and spacious and glowing,
its own sides offering a guide to follow.
But you can only stretch so far,
edge to edge, before the soil crumbles
against the shovel's edge, before
rocks call out a hard resistance.
You had made the empty space
and its final dimensions, the place
for the white roots bright with the hopes
of a new home, bright with the hopes
of fine new roots sent out in all directions.
You had the native soil mounded
on the ground, and in your hands
the wood end of the shovel
ready to fill that wide hole in.

When You Didn't Call

I was on my knees and took
two walnut shells from the base
of the black walnut tree and
put them in my pocket and let them
fit together, against each other,
made sure they stayed there.
Touched them sometimes, setting
them back together where they had
slipped away to let them hold
my worry. Later, my pocket emptied,
at night, I listened through the opening
of the window to hear if you were
calling out, hello there, hello.

When the Eye Can See Again

When the dead branch
fell to pieces on the ground
when the storm winds shook it loose
from the others around it
and when it found you—
just one piece carried down
to your open eye: a fragment caught.
And there's the shake of head that follows,
that blinks the tear down to reddened cheek,
that finds the fold of lip and stops there,
even while another starts to form.
When it clears, when that eye
can see again, when the storm
quiets from the wind, and you,
you are full of your recovery,
then think of all that you can see.

Dandelion

To wear a head of seeds
after such thick gold
is gone has its own relief.
No fragrance or pool
of nectar left, no heavy-
footed bee to plant herself
on solid petals now gone;
now there's space between
each ray that makes
this airy orb, and hours
left to listen to the whispers
of the wind, intact, before
the seeds move off.
To be oneself alone and many—
this is the force that keeps
a hollow stem upright,
this bright head round
and full and, still, not empty yet.

Stranger

Once, before I met you, when we
were strangers, I was wide and alone
as the sky, fine as the grass stems,
slick and dry, I was sunwarmed and
firm as that sea-born shale, brittle and
dark underfoot, and then I floated in the air,
as light as wood ash and water's spray.
When you met me, you pulled me back
to this one shape, so that I could
be with you, settle and be known by you,
so that I was dependable and fixed.
It isn't strange that I have a shadow that
widens still to cover, and lengthens
or shrinks to fit with yours, and
sometimes altogether disappears.

Won't You

give me everything you have:
the beak, the feather, the wing,
the way you sing the morning
song, the way you call out to
mark a territory, the way you nest
and peck at seeds, and come near
among the settled flowers,
your flight: the sweep through
breezy air, the color of black and
red you wear, the feet that hold
on even such a trembling thing
as a thin twig from a tree
that bends its branches down
and how it will be when you let go
and then how you fly again?

Disturb Me

Most of these plants don't
love the sun especially, not yet
growing out of their dumb silences:
a rosette here of leaves that doesn't
budge, a vine that hugs its closed buds
still tight. But the maples
let so much run through them,
as if they were all water, all sap,
all ready, even when the others
can turn their back and sleep.
The grey bark absorbs the sun,
you can feel the heat in it, and
the hidden roots are buried
but they come alive, and you
can taste the sap, how it disturbs
our wintery sleep, and how sweet it is.

The interior text and display type were set in Adobe Jenson, a faithful electronic version of the 1470 roman face of Nicolas Jenson. Jenson was a Frenchman employed as the mintmaster at Tours. Legend has it that he was sent to Mainz in 1458 by Charles VII to learn the new art of printing in the shop of Gutenberg, and import it to France. But he never returned, appearing in Venice in 1468; there his first roman types appeared, in his edition of Eusebius. He moved to Rome at the invitation of Pope Sixtus IV, where he died in 1480.

Type historian Daniel Berkeley Updike praises the Jenson Roman for "its readability, its mellowness of form, and the evenness of color in mass." Updike concludes, "Jenson's roman types have been the accepted models for roman letters ever since he made them, and, repeatedly copied in our own day, have never been equalled."

The cover typeface is Arno. Arno is a serif type family created by Robert Slimbach. It is an old-style serif font, drawing inspiration from a variety of 15th and 16th century typefaces. Slimbach has described the design as a combination of the period's Aldine and Venetian styles.

Silverfish Review Press is committed to preserving ancient forests and natural resources. We elected to print *Territory* on 30% post consumer recycled paper, processed chlorine free. As a result, for this printing, we have saved: 1 tree (40' tall and 6-8" diameter), 499 gallons of water, 293 kilowatt hours of electricity, 64 pounds of solid waste, and 120 pounds of greenhouse gases. Thomson-Shore, Inc. is a member of Green Press Initiative, a nonprofit program dedicated to supporting authors, publishers, and suppliers in their efforts to reduce their use of fiber obtained from endangered forests. For more information, visit www.greenpressinitiative.org.

Cover design by Valerie Brewster, Scribe Typography
Text design by Rodger Moody and Connie Kudura, ProtoType
Printed on acid-free papers and bound by Thomson-Shore, Inc.